'N Laymon's Terms

Hannah -
yo Rock!

'N *Laymon's* Terms

WORDS OF WISDOM

Inspiration to Guide You on Your Life's Journey

LAYMON A. HICKS

ISBN-13: 978-0-9818751-2-5
ISBN-10: 0-9818751-2-2

Cover & Page Design: Carolyn Sheltraw

Printed in the United States of America

This book is available for quantity discounts for bulk purchases.

For additional information about Laymon Hicks, visit him on the web at **www.laymonhicks.com** or email him at **laymon@laymonhicks.com**, or call **1-877-LAYMON0**.

To all who have inspired me.

To all who have allowed me to inspire them.

To all who will allow me to inspire them.

Acknowledgements

Thank you to my Facebook and Twitter friends for helping this book come to life. It was your updates that often gave me the inspiration to come up with some of these sayings.

Thank you to my family and friends for being there with unconditional love, support, and praise.

Thank you to Keisha for your love and support. You have been there every step of the way.

Thank you to my graphic designer, Carolyn Sheltraw for all of your hard work. It has been an incredible journey and I am honored to have you contributing to my success story.

Thank you to Bryan Desloge for your guidance, friendship, and mentorship. I am honored to call you a friend and I thank God for allowing you to be in my life.

Thank you to all my mentors for empowering, encouraging, and elevating me in my life. You all have always pushed me to the next dimension and cared enough to not allow me to settle for mediocrity. Thank you for believing in me.

Most of all I'd like to thank the Father, the Son, and the Holy Spirit. You are the power behind these words, the main source of understanding and inspiration on my journey, and the one who has given me the most.

Introduction

This book has been a dream of mine for quite some time. I have always wanted to have a book full of quotes and aphorisms that could inspire, enrich, and motivate my readers to be more, do more, and have more in their lives. Well, my friend, that is exactly what this book will do. With over 450 quotes and aphorisms, this book was written with the intention to help you get through a rough day. If you read the acknowledgements, you noticed that I thanked my Facebook and Twitter friends. Many of these quotes and aphorisms were created based on many of their updates. So to them, I say thank you!

I am honored that you have this book in your hands right now and I know that it will be a blessing to you. However, I want you to also use this book to bless someone else's life. Do not be afraid to share this book or some of the quotes that you find in this book with others. As a speaker and author, I have found that people are always in need of a word of encouragement and that is why I wrote it. I want this book to be one of your sources of inspiration on your life's journey, but I also want you to use this book as a resource to inspire others.

Look, I did not write this book for you to go through it in one sitting. I created this book for you when you need it most. Therefore, do not just toss this book on the dresser and allow it to collect dust. When you are going through something, this book has the aphorisms to help you see things in a new perspective. They did, and still do, it for me and they did it for the countless friends I have on my social networking sites. Speaking of social networking sites, do not hesitate to share these words with your friends. You never know whose life you can impact with the power of positive words.

My friend, I present to you 'N Laymon's Terms… Words of Wisdom!

Your attitude and actions will keep you from being where you want to be. Get it together.

There is too much purpose for your life for you to just give up. Keep Going. You Got This!

If you are not hungry enough to be a student, then you will never be fully prepared to be a leader.

The party will never get started on time if you continue to wait on others to celebrate who you are.

If He sees the best in you, then maybe you need to wake up and start seeing the best in yourself as well.

How can you expect others to be there, when you aren't there for yourself?

Experience comes from bad decisions and good decisions come from experience. There is a lesson in everything. Pay attention!

**The things that hurt you most
can bring healing to others.
Turn your tests into testimonies.**

We are all born with gifts. Do not wait until Christmas and your birthday to open yours! Bless the world with your talents now.

**You are not a victim. Stop allowing
others to take advantage and
exploit your weaknesses.**

A mirror can crack and shatter, but its broken pieces can still be used.

**To be extraordinary, all you have
to do is put in a little extra.
That is all that is needed.**

While you may not play basketball, you should still be a member of the NBA club. It is where people use their Natural Born Abilities!

**The reason people hate on you is
because they underestimated who you
are and the potential that you had.**

Stop complaining about what you don't have and start celebrating what you do have!

**The time you use hating on others
because of their success is time you
could use to become your own success!**

Your blessing will come when you are truly ready to handle all that comes with it. Do what you got to do so you can have what you want to.

Never become so vulnerable that you ALLOW someone to lead you on. Your name is not Monopoly, so they can stop playing that game!

If you aren't getting what you want out of life, then you need to do something about it. Don't sit around and wait for the right opportunity.

Stop focusing on your failures and missed accomplishments and start celebrating your successes!

Just because someone rejects you does not mean that another person won't accept you. Stop holding on to someone who doesn't want you around!

Some people do not belong in your circle of influence because their influence brings negativity, limited thinking, and irrational decisions!

When you find your self-worth, you ultimately increase your net worth!

Your purpose is bigger than you. Make an impact by using your purpose to bless the lives of others.

If you want the rainbow, then you have to endure the rain. It is always the rain that ends the drought and cultivates the land around you. Get your umbrella and keep on trekking!

In life you have to take it as it happens, but you should try to make it happen the way you want to take it.

There are 40,320 minutes in a month. Why not spend at least ten of those minutes helping someone else? You've got to give a little to get a little.

People will hate on you. That's life. Just use their hate as fuel to propel you to the next level.

Never get down that you are going through something. Remember you are going THROUGH it for a reason-- to get to the other side where things are much better! Keep it moving.

Stop telling people to trust you when you have not proven yourself to be trustworthy.

If you act like nothing and look like nothing, don't be mad when people treat you like nothing!

Some people try to make it seem as though you believe you are all that and a bag of chips, but secretly they wish that their bag of chips was nearly as full as yours!

Who is someone else to tell you who you are and who you are not? Know who you are and be confident in you even when others are not.

Do not be so absorbed by the package that you overlook the product. It's what's on the inside of a person's mind and heart that matters most.

If He only sees the best in you, then you need to do a gut check and see the best in yourself and others as well!

**Some people will build you up today
and quickly cut you down tomorrow.
Be mindful of who you spend
your time with.**

Don't mistake activity with accomplishment. Stop trying to fool people by doing a whole lot of nothing. Get it together!

**Your level of elevation comes with
an increase of temptation. Do not be
tempted to make decisions that will
get you higher because you stepped
on others to get there.**

One's arrogance outshines his or her talents. It is important to remember to be confident in yourself, but not be cocky. You did not get there alone.

There will be things in life that we do not understand. Stop focusing on the uncontrollable and channel your energy to what you can control.

Realize there is more depth to you because of the things that happened to you.

Who you are is not nearly as important as who you can become. Become all that God has intended you to be!

Don't get hung up on what others think you should do. Sometimes they want you to enter a place where they can watch you hang yourself!

You can't go up if all you like to do is lay down. Laziness won't get you anywhere!

Do not use your gifts for self-promotion. Use them to promote others and in return you will be promoted!

Some people think your parents named you April Fool. They think they can treat you like you are a fool & a joke. No ma'am. No sir.

Get in the completion mentality! 5 completed tasks have more power than 15 half-way completed tasks! What have you failed to complete?

Some people will enter your life only to make a quick exit. That's fine. Let them go! Stop trying to fight for relationships and friendships with people who do not want the same.

Put value into who you are, what you do, and who you will become!

Some people, who have a problem with you, actually have a problem with themselves. You are not too confident. It is likely that they are not confident enough!

You win some. You lose some. Although you can be denied of an opportunity, no one can deny you of your determination.

Examine your life and rid yourself of those dream killers and dream stealers. Live your dreams even if those closest to you don't believe in them!

Who you are today is who you were yesterday. Who you are tomorrow is who you were today. What are you doing to be better today than you were yesterday?

Stop being a vulture and living off outdated relationships, goals, and dreams. Be an eagle and go after what is fresh

You do not get to rehearse for the season before you walk into it.

How can you expect others to invest in who you are when you are not willing to invest in yourself?

If you have to question whether or not you are appreciated, then maybe you are not appreciated at all.

There are many people around you who are not worth you telling your dreams to. Be careful and discreet about what you share with others.

Today should not be the only day you are thankful for what life has given you. Every day is a blessing that offers new opportunities.

Stay in your lane and keep your foot on the gas. There is no need to stop when you are on that highway called success!

Friendship isn't required. It is acquired.

Envy can damage you, your relationships, and disrupt your organization. Put just as much focus and energy into yourself as you do into trying to be like other people.

Even at your lowest point, you still have the ability to rise again! No need to be down anymore when you have the ability to go up!

If you don't want your life to be a circus, then you need to stop hanging out with clowns!

If you want to be a lame duck, you will. If you want to be a superstar, you can. Either way, the choice is yours.

Dreams may be delayed, but they aren't denied. Keep working and watch what manifests!

People treat you the way you allow them to treat you. Stop allowing people to treat you like your parents named "Trash".

Stop wasting time on people who do not want to take action. You can't want something for someone who does not want something for themselves.

Always be prepared for the opportunity, you never know when it is going to come!

Stop settling for mediocrity when you have been divinely created to BE YOUR BEST!

In order to enter the unknown, you must be willing to exit that which is known.

If you don't realize your greatest potential, then you can potentially never be great! Recognize your gifts, talents, and abilities.

You are not the sidewalk. Stop allowing people to walk all over you and treat you like you belong under their feet.

You are where you are in life because of the actions that you have taken. If you want to get to greater heights, then you have to take more action.

Just like in the dictionary success comes after fail and failure. Fail greatly so you can achieve greatly.

Who you are is bigger than what you do.

In order to get, you have to give. So give your all no matter what.

If you listen to what THEY say, you will never get where YOU want to go!

Too often when you are confident in whom you are it exposes to others who they are not.

Some people are just added weight that's not needed as you travel to your destination. Get rid of the excess baggage causing you to slow down.

What is for you is for you and no one can't take it away or block it from happening except you! Get to work and get what is yours!

You have to make room for your blessings. It's time to do inventory in preparation for the next year. Get rid of stale relationships and spoiled thoughts.

It's time to cast out the demons known as doubt and denial. You were ordained to receive opportunities. Go for it!

You must put value on the work that you do if you want it to be worth something.

Stop looking for someone else to compensate for the love you should have for yourself. You can't love anyone else, if you do not first love you!

Many of us have walls up in our lives. Do you have friends who care enough to break them down?

Stop worrying about how your dreams will get accomplished and start worrying about what you need to do to get them accomplished.

Some people can't stand you because you have been blessed with gifts and talents that they wish they had!

The start to unlocking your potential begins with your ability to believe in yourself.

You bring so much more value when you let go of your ego.

Stop dressing for success. Dress for work because if you work hard, then you can become a success. Hard work always beats talent, when talent does not work hard!

You will not get every opportunity you go for, but you will get every opportunity that is for you!

There will always be people in life who try to downplay who you are and what you have done. Don't worry about them. Keep your eyes on the prize.

You are not the trash can for someone else's garbage. Get rid of those folks holding you back.

If a person is not worthy of making a DEPOSIT into your life, then why do you continue to allow them to WITHDRAW from your life. If you don't want their negative energy, then stop allowing them to steal your positive energy!

They said, "Drastic times calls for drastic measures." Well, taking drastic measures during drastic times will only leave you drastically desperate, distraught, and depressed in the end.

Stop wasting time on people who claim to want success, but will not do what it takes to get there.

Hard workers carry the look of expectation. When you work hard, you should expect great things to happen!

People with power are intimidated by people with potential. Get ready for some people to hate on you for the potential that you have.

You're right it's other fish in the sea, but some of those fish don't want the bait (BS) you trying to feed them.

Stop waiting for the door to be fully opened before you can walk through it. If the door is cracked, then bust it wide open and walk through.

You would not have major problems if you did not have a major calling on your life. You are gifted enough to handle and get through the problems.

Some people will be intimidated by your intelligence, threatened by your tenacity, and discouraged by your dreams. That's fine. Just be you!

Sometimes you do have to shoot the messenger because they never have anything positive to say. Get away from me with all that negativity!

Stop blaming others for the decisions you made. You can't be a responsible individual if you are not willing to take the responsibility.

The purpose for your life is greater than the problems in your life. Don't allow what's small to stop you from going after what can be big!

Smarts, Talent, Relationships, and Connections can get you there, but it is HARD WORK that will keep you there!

Don't tell me that you can do it. Show me that you can.

You are not a donkey. Stop allowing people to pin their problems on you! Their problem is not your problem. You have your own stuff to deal with.

If you want to get someplace, you have got to give up wanting to get there. In order to achieve, you have got to stop waiting for it to happen and take action now.

You can never accomplish that which you do not work at. Put in the work and watch the return on your investment!

Some people can't understand the anointing on your life, so they do not know how to handle your attitude and altitude.

Don't allow your PR to outweigh your production. Stop allowing the title to lead your life!

If you tell a person that they mean something to you, then show them that. Words can only go so far.

Your future will never be accomplished by what you have lost in the past. Your future is created by using what you have left!

You can't travel to the next dimension of your life with bags that are overweight. Remove the people and things that are causing you to have excess weight on your journey.

Never underestimate your power to make a difference in the world. Someone is in need of the gifts and talents you have to offer.

Never allow your age to derail your ambition!

Are you surrounded by Life Helpers or Life Hinderers? This is your time to WIN! Step up your game and get around the movers and shakers!

In order for an elevator to go up, you must press a button. To get to a higher step on the ladder, you must move your leg. Thus, if you want to go to the next level, you must TAKE ACTION!

It is never crowded on that extra mile. Keep going until you reach your goals and dreams. That is what separates the best from everyone else.

You can't give a person your all, when they don't want to give you nothing. Surround yourself with people who want it just as much as you do.

Being fearful of yourself makes it easier for others to manipulate you into being someone you are not. Embrace who you are.

If you know your value, you have to stop letting people treat you any kind of way. Remember you are an asset and not a liability!

When you understand whose you are, then it is easier to understand who you are! God didn't create a fool.

You are not a game console. Stop allowing others to use you and play you to pass time.

Just like second hand smoke is toxic and can kill you, inhaling someone else's negativity, doubt, and fear can cause mind and purpose cancer and kill your dreams.

We all have our moments when the heat in the kitchen gets a little too hot. The problem is that many of us stay out forever. Get back in and sweat!

Be your best even when no one is looking.

You are not a friend if you only come around when you need something. You are just a user and an abuser of people's time, talent, and wisdom.

If you don't make things happen, then you leave room for others to create them for you!

When you hang around greatness, you too become great!

Some people are like a fire extinguisher. They always trying to put out the fire when the heat is turned up. Know who is for you and who is against you!

Stop being a person who has something to offer someone or an organization and refusing to do it. The best individuals are those who are servants.

Be like an eagle and embrace your storms. Eagles love when storms come because they can go to higher levels.

A degree does not make you. Stop chasing after a piece of paper and have nothing to compliment it!

Whoever said that you had to accept the invitation to the pity party? Wam Bam No Thank You Ma'am!

Live your life as a catalyst and not as a catastrophe. Use your talents and abilities to be a Life Helper, rather than a Life Hinderer!

Shift your mind, your attitude, and your thoughts. Be conscious about your negative thoughts and the words that you say.

Not everyone should receive an invitation to your circle of influence. Some are still stuck thinking inside a box and are not ready for what is in store for you.

If you don't handle yourself with care, then you can't expect anyone else to handle you with care.

**Don't worry about the level of
individual prominence you have
or will achieve. Worry about the
individuals you have or will help to
become better people!**

Learn how to spend quality time with yourself before
trying to spend quality time with someone else. Know
who you are before trying to get to know others!

**We all have the innate ability to
lead, but to lead you must be going
somewhere. So, are you leading in
your own life?**

Many will say to count your blessings today. I say
celebrate your blessings. Regardless of how many
blessings you have received this year or in previous
years, there is one thing for sure... YOU ARE BLESSED.

They say, "Perception is reality." If that is the case, then one should base their perception ON reality.

While companies and organizations are downsizing, they can never downsize your spirit, attitude, and contribution to the world.

You can't satisfy everyone. Learn that NOW. You just can't! Stop being upset that someone disagreed with your decisions or thoughts!

You are not a Jack-In-The-Box. Stop allowing others to stuff you in a box and crank you out when they want to.

You can't change people, but you can change the way you interact with them. You control the situation.

Now is the time to evict the negative people and things that you have allowed to move into your life!

Many people are intimidated by your intelligence, threatened by your tenacity, frightened by your fierceness, and discouraged because of your dreams. Don't let others overwhelm you because you have an opportunity based mindset. Keep moving towards your destiny!

How can you expect to be a success when you do not understand it is okay to fail? Your greatest victories will come as a result of your greatest failures.

Ctrl Alt Delete (the keys to life): Control (ctrl) your future by altering (alt) your lifestyle and deleting (delete) everybody that doesn't want what's best for you.

Take off the sunglasses that are stopping you from seeing how bright your future really is.

If you do not define who you are, you leave space for other people to define you for you. Be confident in who you are!

Stop hanging around people who will only put up with you and start hanging around people who will push you up to the next level!

Go pick up some garden tools so you can get rid of the weeds, trim the unnecessary branches, and cut the grass so you can see the snakes in your life.

People are like airplanes. You only hear about the ones that crash. Recognize someone for the good he or she has done.

**Obstacles are meant to be overcome.
Fear is meant to be conquered.
Success is meant to be achieved.
You got this, my friend!**

Just because someone said you are wrong, doesn't mean that you actually are. Consider whose mouth that came from. It could be a lie!

If people don't have time for you NOW, they won't have time for you LATER! Stop chasing after friendships that you know aren't meant to be.

Find someone who will deposit their time, treasure, and talent(s) into your bank account, so you can do the same for someone else.

If they don't see you as worthy enough to give you a few minutes of their time, then they aren't worthy enough to be in your life. Just like one throws out expired meat and spoiled milk, it's time to get rid of those expired and spoiled relationships and friendships!

Never let someone steal your joy, peace, or happiness. Always be on the pursuit to happiness. The enemy can't win.

Stop stressing! When you stress, you compress your abilities, talents, and gifts!

What others say about you is not near as important as what you say about you. Believe in yourself, even when others do not!

Be honest with yourself. It is possible your actions, attitudes, and associations are keeping you from stepping into the role that God has for you!

Stop chasing after relationships that will leave you unhappy, broke, busted, and disgusted in the end.

Realize your associations can heighten one's hesitation, cease your celebrations, disrupt your determination, and derail your destination.

Start seeing you, for you. Learn to be happy and okay with yourself before you want others to be happy and okay with you. Be happy with who you are!

**Never say anything about yourself
that you don't want to be true.
Speak positively about yourself
and your future!**

You create your character. Others give you a reputation.
Your character is what you really are. A reputation is
what others think you are.

**Your life will never have true meaning
if you choose to ignore the value that
you bring in this world!**

Stop making excuses for doing the things that you
need to do. When you do the things you need to do,
you are free to do the things that you want to do!

**People will summarize your life in one
sentence. Pick yours now!**

As long as you are pleased with your contributions and success, it shouldn't matter that others only celebrate your success for a season.

You can't go back and start a new beginning, but you can go forward and create a new ending.

Now is the time to cast out the demons known as doubt and denial. You were ordained to receive opportunities.

You are not a plastic cup. Stop allowing people to use you and then toss you away when they want to.

People treat you the way they do because they see you put up with the stuff that you do. Do not put up with nonsense and people will not treat you like nonsense!

We were born to be a Chef, to be a creator, but because of reduced vision and limited thinking, many of us remain just cooks!

You do not have to tell the world what you are doing. Just do it and the world will soon find out. When you step into your greatness, you can't be stopped.

Most people can't call you arrogant when they too think they are all that and a bag of chips.

If you don't think you are good enough, then you'll never be good enough. Think positive about who you are and what you can become!

Realize the calling on your life even if others do not recognize it.

Stop being a second rate version of someone else and just be a first rate version yourself! Blaze your own path or someone will create one for you.

Take the time you use to watch television and invest it in yourself and it will not be long before folks are watching you on the television.

Find mentors to guide you on your journey. You can't get to the top alone,

To complain is to give those around you a migraine. The world does not want to hear your complaints. The world wants to see your solutions.

Just because you have freedom of speech, people don't want to hear everything that you have to say.

Surround yourself with people who will tear you down, but build you back up. You want people in your life who are honest in making you your best.

If you want to be a success, then you have to understand it is okay to fail. Your greatest victories will come as a result of your greatest failures.

What others say about you is not near as important as what you say about you. Believe in yourself even when others don't!

If you can control your emotions and control your attitude, you can make it so much farther in life.

Never allow your self perception to get so far down that you allow others to feel free enough to criticize you when they are not gifted enough to assist you. One can't criticize when their life is not in check!

The thing that some people will hate you for is the exact same thing that many will love you for. Don't allow "some" to control your destiny and stop you from accomplishing your dreams.

Those experiences you don't like... either you can be bitter or better because of them. Which will you choose?

You will have haters and sideline spectators. Don't let them get to you. You still have to make a play in this game called Life!

Obstacles will come. You may fail. The question is, do you have the power to get back up? It's too crowded at the bottom. Aim for the top!

People who don't have faith say "If" and those who have faith say "When". Believe it and you can achieve it.

What are you waiting on to live your dreams? Time? Money? Help? You can't accomplish anything by "waiting." Make it happen today!

Do not replicate the mistakes of others and do not imitate those who only want to spectate!

Some people do not value you because they do not recognize how much your gifts, talents, and abilities are worth!

Tired of being broke, busted, and disgusted? Must be willing to give up who you are, so you can become who you want to be

Do what it do because when you do you'll be able to accomplish what you want to.

Limited thinking gets you limited opportunities. There are no limits to what you can accomplish when your thoughts and dedication to your work are aligned with each other.

Stop focusing on your enemies and begin to focus on your destiny!

If you catch on fire, people will jump just to see you burn! So... why not catch on fire with enthusiasm and give them a great show!

Your life is a reflection of what you put up with. If you do not want to be seen as a fool, then do not put up with fools!

It is very much possible to have a miracle even if you have been through some mess.

If you want change, then BE the change. Don't just talk about leadership. Live it!

Many won't support your goals and dreams. Don't get down. Instead use them as fuel as you travel on the highway to success!

Recognize in life that we will all make mistakes. But how you deal with those mistakes is what will determine your ultimate success.

If you were truly friends in the beginning, then one hiccup shouldn't strain your relationship. Learn to forgive and move on.

Your success depends on you and is enhanced by those around you!

Stop asking for advice when you know you do not really want it and you are not emotionally prepared to hear it.

Look, what's yours is yours and what's mine is mine. We are not competing against each other. Stay in your lane and do your own thing!

Stop using your past as an excuse to not create a better future!

If you are not about it, then move out the way. Slacking off gets you no where. Stop taking half steps when the rest of the world is taking full steps.

You can't let the negativity of others drown or affect your positivity!

Sometimes you have to give up some things in order to go up. Evaluate what is really holding you back.

Watch out for people who will dilute your dreams, discredit your destiny, and disregard your determination.

Don't waste time on people that don't really matter. If a person can't respect you and your time, then they don't deserve to be in your life.

If you are tired of being sick and tired, then it is time you wake up and make some real changes to the way you are going about things.

Each of us is a CEO. You are the CEO of You, Inc.! What are your company's profits and losses and how much are you investing in it?

Your passion has to be greater than your purpose. We are all ordained to receive opportunity, but it's the drive and passion that will bring your purpose to life.

You are not a trash pile for people to dump their problems on. Be weary of people who are not looking to find solutions for their own problems.

Stop making a long story short. Celebrate the process so you can enjoy the outcome that much better.

If you don't examine what comes in, then you'll never be satisfied with what comes out!

Don't be a leader and try to take on the qualities of a servant. Be a servant and develop the qualities of a leader.

Stop chasing the dollars and start chasing the change. Dollars will bring you happiness for a while, but the minute you chase change, the minute you chase growth, the minute you chase living your life serving others, then happiness will come for a lifetime!

Stop being blinded by the bad things in life and concentrate on those things that are good.

You are destined to enter a place that eyes have not seen and ears have not heard of. My friend, you are going somewhere.

Remember how you got to where you are and who helped you get there. We all needed help on our journey to success.

If a person is giving you a problem, then you give them the solution. Just like you allowed them to enter your life, you can allow them to exit your life! Hello. Goodbye.

People will say that you act like you know it all. It is not that you know it all. It is just that they don't know enough.

**If you continue to wait on others
to celebrate who you are,
the party will never happen!**

Stop seeing your struggles as struggles and look
at them as opportunities. Learn from your biggest
mistakes. There is a lesson in everything.

**You do not have to give in order to get
in. If you feel like you do, then that's
not the right opportunity for you!**

Do not be content with what you have. Give some away
and you will receive some in return. What you make
happen for others, God will make happen for you!

**One can't be victorious in the
game of life, if they do not
give it all they've got!**

Get out of here... You DON'T know it all and if you think you do, then something is wrong with you!

If all you spew out is stuff that is sugar coated, don't be mad when your teeth fall out!

No one can stop you from being your best unless you want to be stopped. Do not blame others for your mishaps.

Stop allowing people to add drama, negativity, and sour attitudes to your life's collection plate.

Doors to new opportunities are not opened until you are ready to step inside. Get yourself together and watch what unfolds.

**Never underestimate the impact
that you can have on someone.
Even when you do not think
people are watching, they are!**

Don't sabotage someone else's success because you
are holding our own abilities hostage. When you work
hard and use your gifts, you can have your cake and
eat it too.

**You are the match that ignites the
greatness which is standstill in
someone's life. Realize you have
been blessed to bless someone else!**

Being is the process of becoming. In order to BE
someone, you must first BECOME that person.

**Stop telling me what you can do and
what you want to do and just show me.**

Some people just need to be reminded that they are not the Sun. The world does not revolve around them.

Young people are like airplanes, you only hear about the ones that crash. Celebrate those that are still flying high.

If you limit what you are able to do in this world, then there will be someone or some organization that will never reach its full potential. You are the solution to someone's problem.

In order to step into the House of Greatness, all you have to do is open the door and walk in.

The enemy attacks most when you are half way there. Keep pushing! Don't give up!

Stop being so wrapped up in who you are and start focusing on how you can help others become better than who you are.

We already have our gifts present. Some of us have not opened them and others do not know where and how to use them.

They say, "What comes around goes around." Well, success comes around, but it only goes to those who really want it.

Sometimes reality has to slap you in order to remind you to humble yourself and remember that you are not all that and a bag of chips. There is always room for improvement.

If they are telling you someone else's business, do you not think they will tell yours too? Be mindful of who you share your most vulnerable moments with.

The enemy tries to attack when you are at the weakest moments and points in your life. Stay strong and get through the rough times.

Unless you truly understand what it is like to be in that person's shoes, hush your mouth. Keep your two cents and invest it in yourself.

If a person can't handle your life like the valuable commodity that it is, then they aren't worth your time and energy.

Stop trying to do stuff at the 11th hour when you had 10 hours before to get it done!

Your past cannot stop you from a bright and prosperous future. Take your past and use it as the fuel you need to succeed!

Are you the Chef or are you the Cook? A Chef knows how to create something. A Cook only knows how to prepare what has been created.

In order to step into your new opportunity, into your greatness, and into your destiny, you have to STEP -- Start Treating Everything Purposefully.

You can't live high on life with a low self-esteem!

Character is who you really are and reputation is what others say you are. It is time you do a character check up from the neck up.

Stop allowing people to treat your life like a light switch by turning you on and off when they want. YOU own your destiny. Now flip on the switch and LET YOUR LIGHT SHINE!

Stop trying to be like others and be who God created YOU to be!

Be careful about the advice that you receive from others. Most of the time the person giving the advice won't have to deal with what happens after.

Be wise and bold enough to build upon your own dreams because if you do not you will always end up building on someone else's.

Things turn out the best for the people who make the best of the way things turn out.

Stop aiming to be blessed for appearance sake. Appearance can get you there, but it will not keep you there.

A friendship is a bond between 2 people. Don't be fooled. Some may only consider you an associate and will only claim you when they need something.

You are never gifted in isolation as gifted people recognize the gifts in others.

Friendship is not based on longevity, but it is based on availability! Surround yourself with like-minded people to achieve in life. If you hang with the NOTHINGS, you will end up being a NOTHING!

When you were created, you were created with a purpose. Discover yours and live it!

If your significant other does not support your goals and dreams, then maybe you need to reconsider. Don't be limited because of someone else's limited thinking.

When you are the bomb.com, you don't need the spotlight because you already light up the spot!

Some people will dislike you in the process, but when they see the outcome they want to be your best friend. Watch out for fake people.

Someone has the expertise and talent to help you make your dreams come true, but you are missing it because you think you know and have it all.

You better stop barking up the wrong tree before you lose your voice. You know that person is not the one for you!

Vultures like to eat at who you are. Crows like to call you out from who you are. Just hang with the Eagles and soar high!

Never let external issues interrupt your internal peace and joy!

You can only be one place at one time. Be present and engaged where you are!

Stop looking to make an impression and ask yourself how you can make an impact!

Foster an environment that makes others want to give their best.

You are your greatest enemy. Stop allowing your inner critic to stop you from going after what you want.

If you are not careful, you can lose sight of who you are and become who people think you are or who they want you to become. Don't lose the chance of being yourself!

Some people can't handle the altitude of your anointing, so they call you too ambitious and arrogant. They are wrong. You are just hungry for all that is out there for you!

Since the ball is in your court, why not make a slam dunk!

Don't be just enrolled in something. Instead be fully engaged.

Remember where you were and those who came into your life to get you where you are now. You are a fool to believe that this journey called "Life" can be accomplished by yourself.

Stay away from insecure people. They can't handle who you are, so they try to steal and kill your joy and happiness!

You're grown now. Quit playing the childish games!

Stop channeling all of your energy on the outcome and focus on mastering the process. If you can endure the process, the outcome will come!

You can't profit in life if all you do is sit on your assets. Get up and Go get it!

Stop apologizing for what you have been anointed with. Some people do not understand and will never understand the calling on your life.

If you stay focused on what happened yesterday, then you will miss your chance to do something awesome today.

Stop following the status quo and follow your heart. When you do that, you will always end up in a much better place.

Drastic measures due to drastic times will only leave you drastically desperate, distraught, and depressed in the end.

Sometimes the right thing to do is the hardest thing to do.

If you psych yourself out before the opportunity comes, then when it does appear, you will not be prepared or know how to handle it!

Your positivity has to be greater than anyone's negativity. You have to have faith even when others live under that cloud of doubt.

If you are locked up by limitation, it is time to break out and advance in life.

Every package has on it a warning label. Be sure that you are prepared for the effects of that package. Some of us are not prepared to handle the product.

Sometimes you are told "no" so that you can realize the bigger picture-- that there is something greater going to happen in your life!

Why should someone's expectations of you be high, when the expectations of yourself are low?

You build who you are by building up others.

You have to be like a computer keyboard and DELETE some folks out of your life, SHIFT your thinking, END meaningless relationships, and ESCAPE to a place where you feel comfortable to START living your dreams!

Don't allow anyone to have so much authority over your life that they begin to block you from growing, developing, and having happiness!

Greater blessings come when you bless those who can't reciprocate! Be a servant leader.

People are quick to say you can't handle the truth. What they fail to realize is that their "truth" is just a bunch of lies!

If you allow them, people will use and abuse your time, energy, and resources. It's time to take ownership over what's YOURS!

Strive for perfection as it creates improvement. No, we can ever be perfect, but we can be improved. Think Big. Act Big. Be Big!

Invest your time and energy into others who can provide a return on investment that will make you proud and happy that you have given your all.

If you don't like the way something is, then what are you doing to try and change it? Otherwise be quiet, get with the program, or jump off the bandwagon!

If you don't invest in yourself, then why should anyone else invest in you?

Put your destination in your life's GPS system. If you must detour, remember it will recalculate and still get you there.

You can never get where you want to go, if you are unwilling to leave where you are!

If you can't articulate what you want, then don't expect others to know what you want!

You are not a grocery store. Stop allowing people to drop in when they need or want something.

The players that make the most impact are the ones that are in the game and not sitting on the bench. GET IN THE GAME!

It does not matter how many blessings you have received, what matters is that you are blessed. Today, be thankful!

Some people will treat you like a penny and think that you bring no value. However, the last time I checked, pennies have value too!

If you say you're done with "it," then be done! Stop going back and forth.

You can have more degrees than a thermometer. It doesn't make you smart. Aim to gain wisdom because that's what will get you through.

Education or not, you still have to work hard to get where you want to go. Keep moving!

Being YOU never goes out of style. You don't have to keep up with the Joneses!

Don't live your life trying to please others. Live your life trying to please God. In the end, that's what really matters!

Be bold in your dreams. Be bold in your actions. Be bold in life! It's Your Time To Shine!

Stop holding yourself hostage because of your limited thinking. Break out of captivity, be free, go after what you want, and don't look back!

Just because you have freedom of thought and speech, it doesn't mean you have to think and speak negatively.

If someone is denying you of being your best, then it is time to approve them to get out of your life and get on with theirs!

Stop talking about it and be about it!

Get away from the dream killers and connect with dream fulfillers!

You are not a basketball game. Stop allowing people to cross you over, steal your joy, and take shots at you when they want to.

There are too many resources and opportunities in this world for you not to be living or moving towards your goals and dreams. Seriously.

You will always be at the bottom when you don't expect to make it to the top!

You can't give what you don't have. Stop making excuses. If you don't have it, you just don't have it!

When you get there, everything you need will be there. Follow your path, be determined, and stay faithful.

Let go of those artificial friendships that are draining and don't bring the value you deserve in your life! You need authentic friendships.

Use the hateration as motivation to keep going. People will reject you and overlook you. They just don't realize you are the bomb.com!

Be someone known as an individual who works hard rather than a person who hardly works.

You are like a pencil without an eraser. You can't erase your past, but you can write your future.

You are about to give birth to your dreams. The trials you are experiencing are the contractions. Keep pushing. Keep pushing. You are almost there!

If you're all that and a bag of chips, you don't have to tell the world. It will notice you. Let your work speak for itself!

If you fall seven times, you should stand back up eight times!

Sometimes you have to say no to others, so you can say yes to yourself! If you don't value your time and energy, why should anyone else?

How can you love someone else when you don't love yourself? Stop looking for someone to overcompensate for not being able to love yourself.

Surround yourself with people who want it just as bad as you do. You can never be great if you hang with people whose mindset is not great.

That person getting you all worked up... Yes, it is time to send them to the unemployment office.

If you put as much energy into yourself as you do into following the lives of other celebrities, then you too could become a star!

Too many people are impregnated with the dreams and goals of others. It is time to give birth to YOUR dreams and goals!

Your opposition is because you are productive. If you were not productive, then the enemy would not be trying to attack you.

Don't slow down during the last leg of the race. It is then when you must finish strong! It can be hard, but be strong. You've got this!

The enemy wants you to lose and every time you reach the top, he tries to convince you that you do not belong there. My friend, you do belong!

People will value who you are when YOU begin to value who you are!

Age is a state of mind. You are never too young or too old to make a difference and impact in the world. Use your gifts and talents today!

Stop seeing who you are and start seeing who you are becoming. You are better than your worst mistake. You are also better than what you think is your best.

Stop looking to man to validate you. Validate yourself and watch what follows!

The time to act on your dream is NOW. Stop waiting for the right time. If you continue to wait, there will NEVER be a right time.

Finish the job. Not following through can lead to the lost of confidence in you and your abilities!

Don't aim to change someone. Aim to inspire them to change themselves. Change begins with one's self. Must change yourself before you do others.

Stop itching to have success and you are not even willing to scratch for it!

There will be those that do not believe in your goals and dreams. There will be those that attempt to limit your success. There will even be those that question your abilities, talents, gifts, skills, and knowledge. Do not worry about proving them wrong. Continue to do you and watch how others who are meant to be in your life flock to you because they believe in you.

When you are marked for greatness, you are a magnet for criticism. Do not allow criticism to confine the magnitude of your dreams.

Do not travel through life working on someone else's job, only to leave your dreams unemployed. Live YOUR dreams!

You can go as far as you are willing to go. So, in that case, give until you can't give anymore so you can get until you can't get anymore.

Stop spending $500 worth of your time on a $5 problem. In other words, stop giving attention to people and things that don't really matter!

Some people will take a stand against you because they rather live their life sitting down. Never allow a lazy person to stop you from being active!

**You can never seize what you
are unwilling to go after.
If you want it, go get it!**

Some "friendships" do nothing but cause you
hardships. It's time to rid yourself of those people who
are keeping you from moving forward!

**If you are sick and tired of being sick
and tired, then it is time to regroup,
refocus, and release yourself from
what's holding you down.**

Instead of focusing on what gifts and talents you do
not have, focus on what God has given you and be
YOUR best!

**Get rid of the parasites in your life.
Stop allowing people to be a leech and
suck all the energy out of your life!**

Some people can't recognize their blessings because they are too busy wishing they had the blessings that others have received. Be thankful for what you have!

You are where you are today because of your mind and you will be where you are tomorrow because of your mind.

Stop hanging with Life Hinderers and start associating with Life Helpers!

Some people will say that you are arrogant because they are upset with the level of confidence you have in yourself!

Stop allowing yourself to fall in the trap of complacency. If you want to go up, then you have to get up!

If your "friend" is jealous of whom you are, what you have, and who you are becoming, then that's not a friendship. That's just hatership. You better believe they are griping and sniping about you to someone else!

People will hate on you. That's a given. You just do not stoop to their level. Take the high road while they keep living the low life.

Sometimes you have to give without the expectation of getting. Remember, you were blessed to bless others.

You will get where you want to be when it becomes unacceptable to stay where you are!

**Do not be so caught up in your
gift that you forget to wrap
a present for someone else.**

If all you do is recognize the failure in others, then
chances are you are a failure yourself! Step your game up!

**Some people are not genuinely
interested in knowing what you do.
They are only interested in knowing
what you do, so that they can
stop you from doing it!**

You won't be liked by everyone and everyone won't like
all that you do. Never allow someone to bring you down
so low that you forget how high you can go.

**How can you quit when you've been
anointed to go get it? Go for it!!!!**

A true friend understands your past, accepts you for who you are, and believes in your future.

Don't invite someone to your inner circle when they refuse to step outside of their little box. Stop wasting time on people who claim to want success, but won't do what it takes to get there!

People's expectations of you will always be higher. Don't stress yourself out trying to meet them.

Stop trying to find people to complete you and find people that will compliment you!

You say you done, but yet you running back like a helpless addict.

No one has been blessed with the total package. Anyone who has done great things has had the help of others. Do not be afraid to ask for help.

You are not a circus. Stop allowing others to view you as "for entertainment purposes only".

Your growth is parallel to your ability to learn from your failure just as much as you do from your success.

When you understand how much you are worth, then it becomes easier for you to realize the value you bring to this world.

If you put yourself before your team, you manipulate them. If you put your team before yourself, you motivate them!

Winners are losers who gave it one more try! Be persistent in pursuing your goals and dreams!

DO YOU! All that is for you will fall into place. If you constantly compare yourself to others, you will wear yourself out and tear up any possibilities of accomplishing your goals or dreams.

Don't be so caught up in the difficulty of the journey that you forget where you are going!

If you constantly live your life worried about what others think of you, then you'll never end up where you want to be! Do you.

You were placed on this Earth to be the spark that will light someone's fire inside.

Let go of those energy vampires and find you some energy magnifiers. Who will help increase your energy so you can become a better individual?

Stop claiming a friendship with people who are not there when you need them. Friendship is based on availability NOT longevity!

Leadership is not all about the galore and the glamour. It is about remaining true to your values, inspiring people, building up those around you, following through on your plan, and much more. Learn to lead yourself before leading others.

Listen to your inner voice. It may guide you to the answer you have been looking for.

Sometimes you have to be knocked down in order to realize that you have the potential to go up!

Do not be so caught up in the award that you forget the value that you bring. You do not need an accolade to show you that you are doing your thing.

Stop wasting time on people and things that have no meaning to whom you are and where you are trying to go in life.

Don't be mad that you can't get out the mud hole when you are the one who wanted to dibble and dabble in the mud. You knew you shouldn't have been messing around with that person.

Some of us are so blessed that we can barely hold on to anything.

The invisible can become visible when you set goals, believe in them, and take action!

You can't travel boldly into your future with your gas tank on E. Take time out for yourself to refuel and get rejuvenated so you can enjoy the rest of the ride!

Stop wasting your valuable time wondering if they are going to call or text. You'll never be able to get that time back. Don't be a fool!

Acknowledge the success in your life, but realize there is always room for improvement.

You can't want success if you refuse to work at it. The outcome does not happen without a process!

Why aim low when there are no limits in life? Seize the resources and opportunities that the world has to offer.

Stop allowing people to PUSH you to a place where you feel like you have to PULL your hair out! You are in control of the situation!

It is not if you make it, but it is when you make it! You are destined for greatness.

There can't be elevation without complication. The struggle now is meant to prepare you for the success later!

What you sow, you will reap. Well, in that case, it is time to start sowing GREATNESS, so you can reap GREATNESS! Go get it!!!

**Sell the steak and not the sizzle!
Don't worry about telling people
what you are capable of. Just let
your actions do the talking.**

When others throw bricks at you, use them to build or strengthen the foundation that will elevate you to the next level of success.

**You are not a prisoner of your past.
Break out of that mental
and environmental jail cell
and begin living free today!**

It's time to let those people who are adding drama and negativity to your life exit, so that those who want to add value can enter!

There are 31,536,000 seconds in a year. Why not dedicate a few of them to tell someone "thank you," "I love you," or "I appreciate you!"

Tomorrow is not promised, but you are here today. Therefore, make the most of it.

Within an acorn is a strong oak tree. Within a cocoon is a beautiful butterfly. Within an egg is a gorgeous swan. So, the question is what is within you? The answer: Greatness and Brilliance.

Someone may be anointed, but it does not mean they are authentic.

You can go after your dreams. You can go after your goals! Never let anyone tell you differently! The road may be long and the journey may get hard, but don't give up. Obstacles are meant to make you stronger and that much more prepared for the opportunity!

You will never have high results when you are stuck on meeting low expectations!

Today is the day to move from observation to participation. Go out into the world and live your dreams and stop watching others live theirs.

You have to be your biggest cheerleader! You have to believe it is possible before anyone else will.

**There comes a time where some
people are not worth your attention.
Stop focusing on people who leave
you stressed, dejected, and not
able to be your best!**

You are the CEO of YOU, Inc. Don't be afraid to hand someone the pink slip. Not everyone deserves a promotion.

**It's not about time management.
It's YOU management. When you
manage who you are, your life
will be so much better.**

If you aren't ready for success, then move out the way. There are a ton of people who are.

If you don't want to move up in life, don't be mad or hate on those that are putting in the work to make things happen. Get with the program

Some will call you a friend, but really you are only a friend when they need something from you. Be weary of who you allow into your space.

Don't compromise who you are for others. In the end, you will be let down, upset, and far removed from your authentic self!

Bad habits are like a comfortable bed...Easy to get into, but hard to get out of.

Remember it is progress, not perfection.

Just like the swine flu spread, leadership should spread because it's about inFLUence. How are you spreading your inFLUence?

Your appearance does not determine your ability.

Too many people overvalue what they are not and undervalue what they are.

Some may say that you lack experience. That's fine. Never ever allow someone to say that you lack ambition! Go after what you want.

There is a problem that only you have been anointed to solve. Remember you are the prescription to someone's pain!

**Some people have become fluent
in speaking negativity and talking
about others. Watch out!!!
Those are two languages that
you do not need to learn.**

If you don't want to be treated like a cartoon character,
then stop acting like one! It's simple as that!

**Be your own NBA star and use your
Natural Born Abilities! Think Big.
Act Big. Be Big!**

People say you are arrogant. It is really just your
confidence bumping against their insecurities. Do you!

**Learn from the mistakes of others,
so you can ascend to new heights,
levels, and dimensions!**

Everyday is a new day to bless someone new. What's your random act of kindness today?

Don't hurt yourself trying to jump on someone else's bandwagon only to be disappointed with where the ride is going!

You can't move forward if you are stuck in park. Put that thing in drive and GO.

You cannot become what you want to be by remaining what you are!

Tell them they can take their silly games somewhere else. Tricks are for kids!

You do not need people to authenticate and validate who you are. All that matters is that you accept who you are.

Stop trying to impress and just express who you really are!

You can't make your dreams a reality if you are too busy and caught up in watching others accomplish theirs. Don't be a spectator. Be a participator!

Your associations determine your destination. Who are you associated with and where are they taking you?

Why wait for the grand prize when smaller prizes will do? It is the small steps that lead you to the giant journey.

Some people will treat you like a worthless check because they do not see the value that you bring.

Your elevation is shaped by your determination!

Your name is not Monopoly, Spades, Uno, XBOX, or PS3. People will try to play you like you are a game. Watch out for them. Be one step ahead

Your name is not Halloween. Stop allowing people to use your life as a place to trick-n-treat. Tricking you into believing that they care and treating you like a worthless check!

Don't expect success if you are unwilling to work for it. The small steps you take now will lead you to the big opportunities later!

If you don't communicate what you want, don't expect someone to just automatically know what you want!

Some people have an issue with you not because of things you have done to them, but what you have done to improve yourself. They don't want you to have your cake and eat it too!

There is a time and a place for everything. Well, this is the time and this is the place for you to get up and go after what you want!

You do not have to wait for a raise. Raise yourself! Raise your standards. Raise your confidence and everything else will fall into place.

Be a leader that allows others to shine and not feel like their greatness is being suppressed.

Allow your actions to articulate your dreams and vision!

Sometimes it is not our destination that we need to change. It could very well be our direction. Be mindful of the direction that you are headed in.

You can't get a refund when you sell yourself short. Don't be afraid to celebrate who you are and what you have accomplished in your life!

You breathe the same air as a billionaire. You have the same amount of hours in a day as a millionaire. So, what is stopping you from being great?

Just because you hold a title or position does not mean that you are greater than the next person. Remember who you were before the fame.

Know who you are dealing with. A person can't bring stress to your life unless you allow them to.

Stop rushing to your goals and just enjoy the process. Life is not a 100 yard dash, it's a marathon that must be jogged and not sprinted! For if you sprint, you will quickly tire.

People who say that you are not worthy of getting what is yours are just mad that they cannot have what you are getting. Watch out for them!

In order to become relevant, you have to let the irrelevant things go.

You are the medicine to someone's headache.

Success lies in our daily habits. What do you do daily to be a better individual, friend, brother, sister, student, or employee?

If you are willing to quickly give up on yourself, then don't be upset when someone else gives up on you. You have to want it for yourself first.

Watch out for people who have not advanced in life. Their goal may be to make sure that you do not advance in life.

Don't just want to be successful, actually be it! You can want all you would like, but you have to take action to get it.

In order to enter into your destiny, you have to exit those things that are holding you back.

Stop seeing the glass as half empty or half full and just see it as FULL. If you want the best, then you have to expect the best.

Others won't talk about how big of a camp fire you built, but how well you kept others warm. That's the price of leadership!

Realize those people that are holding you down. Relieve them of that duty. Then, replace them with people who can help you go up!

Some people do not know how to handle your talents and abilities because they do not understand the sacrifice that you have made.

**Stop riding on the coat tails of
someone else. It is time that
you invest in your own coat!**

Grab a hold to the hand of someone who is where you want to be and take the hand of someone trying to get where you are. Let's all go up together!

**If you do decide to limit anything
in life, it should be to limit your
stinkin' thinkin, limit your destructive
dialogue, and limit the other fumes
that prohibit you from being your
best all the time!**

So many opportunities have been thrown your way that you ignore the ones you need the most thinking there will be more.

Decide today that you will be on a mission because if you don't, you will become the mission of someone else! Discover your purpose folks.

Every exit is an entry to somewhere else. One man's garbage may be another one's treasure.

Stop trying to be better than the next person and just be better than your current self. You are your greatest competition!

The reason people talk behind your back is because you are in front of them. Realize you will always have haters, but never stop moving forward.

The difference between where you are and where you are going is how you have applied yourself in the process!

Never underestimate the difference you can make in the world. You never know whose life you can brighten with your smile or whose life you can impact with your words!

If you want this year to be your year, then start making each day YOUR day!

Some people can't catch a blessing because it is too much being thrown their way.

Don't expect anything when you haven't done anything.

If the door has been shut, that means that YOUR door is still open.

Never allow someone else to dictate who you are or who you can become. No matter the obstacles or challenges, live your dreams!

GAGA YOUR WAY TO GREATNESS!!!!!! Be unique. Be different. Be bold.

Don't ask a no question if you want a yes answer.

The difficulties and struggles of today are the price we must pay for the accomplishments and victories of tomorrow.

Beyonce said "Let me upgrade you."
It's time you start upgrading yourself.
Stop looking to others to validate you!
You're a winner!

Never allow where you are to dictate WHO you are. You are bigger and better than your environment.

Some people will encourage your
dreams and others will try to suppress
them. Surround yourself with people
who want you to succeed.

You can't lead others if you do not know how to lead yourself. Know who you are and the vision and mission for YOUR life!

All trees have roots.
Who is helping you grow?

If you want to go up, you have to get up! Get Up from limited thinking, negative environments, sour friendships, and all that is stopping you from moving up.

Don't be satisfied with just one success and don't give up after one failure! Keep progressing and moving forward.

The anointing on your life is so overwhelming that it is hard to articulate to and get buy-in from those who are non-believers!

Stop blocking your dreams from happening by allowing fear to grow bigger than your faith.

Stop allowing people to be that gnat in your life. Stop allowing people to bug you so much that it stops you from being your best.

**Be real with yourself. Some people
you claim to be your friend
do not see you as a friend.**

Never allow others to dictate your destiny and dreams.
You control the brush that is used to paint your future.
Use it accordingly!

**Be thankful for the gifts, talents,
and abilities that have been
bestowed upon you. Now, go use
them and bless others.**

You made it. Congratulations. Now do not forget all of
those people that helped you get there.

**It's about who you know.
It's about what you know.
It's also about who knows you.**

Your "will" has to be greater than other people's "might". When others say they "might" do something. Show the world that you "will" do it.

Who you are should be greater than who you are and who you will become should be greater than who you are. You have got to keep growing if you want to become the person you dream to be.

Life without effort is like leaving a gold-mine and coming out empty handed! Don't go through life thinking, "What if I had done..."

You will never be treated like a hot commodity when you walk around with a cold heart and a cold shoulder.

Stop giving value to people and things that do not add value to who you are!

**Low expectations will never
give you the opportunity to
achieve high results!**

Stop being sick and tired of being sick and tired. In order to get there, you had to make a choice. So make the choice to be well and lively!

**Never base your decisions off advice
from people that don't have to deal
with the consequences!**

Live life as a participator and not a spectator. Work on your dreams today!

**Some people will hate on you and always
find fault with what you are doing when
you are out there making it happen. Do
not worry about them. Just do you!**

If you are done with it, then be done with it. You can never step into your greatness if you keep holding on to your past.

You are annoyed by people because you allow them to annoy you.

When you have not done anything, you should not expect anything. If you want it, then you have to go get it!

Sometimes if you want to see a change for the better, you have to take things into your own hands.

Stop running out of breath trying to be in competition with others. Use the energy to better yourself and watch what unfolds.

If you are not willing to work for it, then you do not expect it to happen.

In life, you must know when things have run its course. Therefore, it is time to let go of the things that are holding you back.

If you want to be your best, then you have to start giving your best.

About the Author

Enriched, Elevated and **Empowered** is exactly what the youth and adult audiences feel after listening to one of **Laymon A. Hicks** transformative talks. A Bachelors and Masters Degree graduate of The Florida State University, Laymon was a pivotal player on campus, serving as Student Body President which entailed him managing and overseeing a **$10.3 million** budget as well as cultivating campus leaders.

Laymon A. Hicks is also the author of *A Treasure Chest of Motivation: 8 Jewels of Wisdom for a Young Adult's Success* and co-author of *Unleash the Passion for your Purpose,* and I*gnite Your Dreams: How to Build and Accelerate Your Life as a Top Notch Student.*

Hicks believes in paving the way for others younger than him, so they too can use their gifts, talents, and abilities. As a result, he founded the Laymon A. Hicks Scholarship Fund which funds an annual scholarship to a first generation student entering a two or four year college or university.

To bring Laymon A. Hicks to your school, conference, or organization please visit www.LaymonHicks.com or contact him at laymon@laymonhicks.com or 877-529-6660.